EDWARD ELGAR

the sketches for

SYMPHONY NO. 3

elaborated by

ANTHONY PAYNE

Full Score

BOOSEY & HAWKES

London · New York · Berlin · Sydney

Facsimile of the manuscript of the opening page of Elgar's
Symphony No. 3, one of the few passages he completed in full score.

Facsimile of a page of Elgar's sketches for the third movement. Two ideas are represented: the first four systems show the first main theme of the movement, commencing at bar 7 (page 87) in the printed score; the bottom system shows a harmonic sequence used later in the movement, commencing at bar 31 (page 91).

AN INTRODUCTION BY ANTHONY PAYNE

I first came across the sketches for Elgar's Third Symphony at the end of W. H. Reed's book *Elgar as I Knew Him*. The majority of the most important pages are reproduced there in facsimile and I was immediately fascinated by the power and vitality of the music. It simply leapt from the page, and although most of the sketches were in short score, with only a few instrumental indications, I immediately began to hear orchestral sounds in my head.

I knew that on his deathbed Elgar had placed an embargo on attempts to complete the work, on what he called "tinkering" with it; but I felt this could not prevent me from musing over the sketches in the privacy of my room, and I used to follow them through aided by Reed's account of how he played them on his violin with Elgar at the piano. It was music that seemed to me to show Elgar in inspirational flight, and it gave the lie to received opinion that he had become a spent force after the death of his wife.

The history of the Symphony has been well documented, but it is worth repeating the basic facts. Elgar's old friend George Bernard Shaw had often badgered the composer about producing a third symphony, and early in 1932 he renewed his attack, suggesting that the BBC might be persuaded to commission it. This time Elgar half rose to the bait. He had recently orchestrated Chopin's Funeral March, and when he was asked by a critic if the rest of Chopin's sonata could be orchestrated to make a symphony, he replied that he would sooner write one of his own.

The affair snowballed: newspapers got hold of the story, Shaw cajoled the BBC, and Elgar actually spoke of having "written" the Symphony after he had been quizzed at that year's Three Choirs Festival. Composers can mean many different things when they speak of having "written" something, but we can probably take it that a lot of the Symphony had already come into focus in his mind. All that he needed was time to put it down. Eventually, in December, the BBC announced officially that they had commissioned the Symphony, and from then on we may take it that Elgar approached the work with deep seriousness.

Throughout what was to be the last complete year of his life, he put parts of the work down on paper. It was sometimes an extended section, sometimes just a chord progression, and Reed tells us of intense sessions they spent together on the music. Elgar would pound away at the piano, and exhort Reed to tear his heart out on the violin. The composer had an extraordinary way of working, jumping from movement to movement as the spirit took him. It was as if he was shaping the various pieces of the jigsaw, before fitting them all together. Ideas sometimes came to him outside the context of a tempo, for instance, and one, clearly marked 'scherzo', eventually ended up in the slow movement. By the same token, themes from earlier years were pressed into service — ideas for *The Last Judgement*, for instance, an oratorio which never saw the light of day, and episodes from his incidental music for Laurence Binyon's historical drama *Arthur*, which he had composed a decade before. Critics have held this against the Symphony, but there is no real reason why ideas cannot be re-allocated in this way, especially when they are as impressive as they are here: the practice goes back to Bach and beyond. Elgar's borrowed themes became part of an overall vision, fused together by the intensity of his creative thought.

Tragically, however, his labours were to be of no avail. In October 1933, after an exploratory operation, cancer was diagnosed and he quickly went into a decline. He composed no more, and in February 1934 he died, leaving over 130 pages of sketches for the unfinished Symphony. I believe these pages contain the vestiges of an inspired work, yet they seem to have aroused little interest until comparatively recently. Elgar's reputation sank to a low ebb in the period after his death, which partly accounts for this; but even when the sketches were explored, few imaginative insights seemed forthcoming.

My own involvement with them, dating from late 1972, did not immediately lead to any serious work. Contemplating the sketches was merely an intermittent hobby, and years would pass by in which I paid them no attention. But in 1993 all that changed. Paul Hindmarsh of BBC Manchester telephoned to ask whether I would be interested in putting the sketches into some sort of shape for workshop performance. I jumped at the idea: it would compel me to collect my thoughts and systematically write down the many connecting links between sketches and extensions of them which I had envisaged over the years. I took little note of Paul's caveat, that the BBC would first have to obtain permission for the project from the copyright owners: on the spur of the exhilarating moment I completed the Scherzo, for which the sketches supplied all the material, and then managed to write out a complete exposition for the Adagio by means of jigsaw-puzzling with the sketches. Reed's book, which had been of considerable help in remembering the order of events in the Scherzo, did not help with the Adagio. He seemed not to know how the movement opened, although the sketches make it clear, nor was he aware of the order in which the main subjects were to appear. All this had to be worked out by educated guesswork and intuition.

By now the BBC had sent me photocopies of the complete sketches, which were housed in the British Library, and I discovered that Reed had overlooked many pages of considerable interest. With the bit firmly between my teeth, and encouraged by a scrap of developmental music I had discovered in the complete sketches, I began to see how I could complete the Adagio. I forged ahead and wrote the last bar on February 23 1994, only later realising, with a considerable frisson, that this day marked the sixtieth anniversary of the composer's death. I thought at this point that I had achieved all that was possible, for Elgar had only written down the exposition and recapitulation of the first movement, while the material for the Finale enabled one to assemble the exposition and no more.

All of this was shortly to become of academic interest, however, because the Elgar family, who controlled the copyright to the sketches, came to the decision after much deliberation that they could not allow work to continue on the project. They felt in all honesty that their great-uncle's deathbed wish could not be over-ruled. I sympathised with their stance, but was, of course, deeply disappointed. I had begun to feel as involved with the Symphony as if it had been a piece of my own.

At this stage I put everything back into my bottom drawer, thinking rather dejectedly that I would probably never return to the Symphony. But the saga continued to unfold. The family said that they had no objection to the idea of a radio programme about the sketches, as long as my 'tinkerings' were not alluded to. Accordingly I went ahead and recorded a talk for the BBC in March 1995. It caused something of a stir, and convinced many who had previously underestimated the sketches that the Symphony would have been of the highest quality. I returned home from the recording thinking that this really was the end of the affair, but fate had other ideas. Next day, when taking a final look at the sketches, prior to packing them away for good, I quite suddenly discovered the key to completing the first movement — the very thing I had just said was impossible in my radio talk. The idea struck with the force of a lightning bolt: I recognised that four pages of faintly outlined fragments I had previously discounted were in fact intended for the development section. Plunging in at the deep end, I completed the development and the related coda in a couple of weeks. Despite the family's embargo, I felt that I owed it to Elgar to finish as much as I could whilst the spirit was upon me. Maybe posterity would find a place for my realisation, even if circumstances were currently against it.

It was now the summer of 1995, and I had to put the Symphony aside for the time being while I completed a commission of my own. But after the exhilarating experience of finishing the first movement, I felt for the first time that I could perhaps complete the whole Symphony. It seemed as if I was being impelled by forces outside myself, and again fate took a hand: the Elgar family began to change their minds. Realising that the sketches in Reed would in any case come out of copyright in 2005, allowing anyone to 'tinker', they decided to take control of the situation. It was a few months before they reached a consensus, but finally a unanimous decision was taken to commission from me a complete version of the Symphony, and in August I began to write out in full orchestral score all that I had so far done. That is, the first three movements and the beginning of the Finale. It was while doing this that I became more consciously aware of the overall sweep of the Symphony. It was different in its sheer breadth of emotion from any of his other symphonic works. There was the raw vigour and magic lyricism of the opening movement, the use of a lighter manner in the second which went far beyond his established symphonic practice, and the searing intensity of the Adagio, tragic in its import, while the Finale revealed a world of chivalric action and drama.

All this was at the back of my mind as I faced the last and greatest obstacle: nowhere did Elgar leave a hint as to how his Symphony was going to end. I had to compose the whole of the development section and the coda, much as in the first movement, but without the helpful pointers, and I had to envisage the work's ultimate goal — the toughest assignment of all, involving visionary concepts if I was to be true to Elgar's creative bravery. It was not even certain what basic structure Elgar had in mind for his Finale, although I felt that the breadth of the expository material in the sketches pointed towards a sonata form. This could be enriched by incorporating into the development a ravishing G minor interlude whose placing in the movement is not precisely indicated by the sketches. As it now stands, the passage seems to have strayed from some rondo sub-stratum and yields a structural ambivalence which I hope is worthy of Elgar's symphonic thought.

As for the Symphony's closing pages, I decided to dare all in honour of Elgar's unpredictability. What if he had thought to place the haunting repetitions of *The Wagon Passes* from his recently completed *Nursery Suite* into a broader symphonic context? The Finale's main subject actually suggests this kind of treatment, and it would lead the music away into some new visionary world, spanning the years between the composer's death and my attempted realisation of his sketches. I trusted my intuition and went ahead and wrote.

EDWARD ELGAR

Edward Elgar was born in 1857 at Broadheath in Worcestershire, and lived the greater part of his life in the countryside that he loved; he died at his home in Worcester in 1934. Although his family was a musical one, Elgar was entirely self-taught as a composer, and he first established himself as a music teacher and professional violinist. His published compositions during the 1890s were in the English oratorio tradition, but it was with the orchestral *Enigma Variations* of 1899 that he achieved international recognition. He was to return to oratorio several times, most notably with The *Dream of Gerontius* (1900), but he never completed the third part of a subsequent trilogy on the Apostles. He turned instead to symphonic works — the two symphonies of 1908 and 1911, the Violin Concerto (1910), the symphonic study *Falstaff* (1913), and in 1919 the Cello Concerto. He was a highly skilled composer of lighter music, including the five *Pomp and Circumstance* marches. After the death of his wife in 1920 he wrote very little, although his last years saw an attempt to return to large-scale composition, including an opera. Elgar was one of the first great composers to record his own music, and he conducted many recordings between 1914 and 1933, supervising a final recording session by telephone from his bed a month before he died.

© Colin Matthews, 1998

ANTHONY PAYNE

Composer, writer, broadcaster, and animateur, Anthony Payne is one of the most respected British musicians of his generation. Born in London in 1936, he began composing as a schoolboy — though after reading music at Durham University, he suffered a period of creative uncertainty as he struggled to integrate the innovations of the Continental avant-garde with the romanticism of such early 20th-century British composers as Elgar, Delius and Vaughan Williams for which he felt an affinity. Only with the completion in his early thirties of the *Phoenix Mass* (1965–72) did he at last sense "the natural emergence of a new manner, long sought after but previously only partly envisaged".

Since then, however, he has accumulated an imposing catalogue of some 50 works in all genres except opera. In addition to his two major commissions for the BBC Proms — *The Spirit's Harvest* (1985) and *Time's Arrow* (1990) — his orchestral output includes the Delius paraphrase *Spring's Shining Wake* (1981) and the autobiographical *Orchestral Variations — The Seeds Long Hidden* (1994), while his ensemble music ranges from the constructivist String Quartet (1978) to the much-played fantasy-sextet *A Day in the Life of a Mayfly* (1981).

Meanwhile, Payne has continued to promote the understanding of music through a multiplicity of activities: as author of books on Schoenberg and Frank Bridge, as music critic for the *Daily Telegraph*, *The Independent* and *Country Life*, as contributor to a range of publications from *Tempo* to the *New Grove Dictionary*, as a teacher in universities as far afield as Australia and the United States, and, not least, as a frequent broadcaster. In addition to years of service to the Society for the Promotion of New Music, he continues to guide the questing young ensemble, Jane's Minstrels, which he co-founded in 1988 with his wife, the soprano Jane Manning, as a practical expression of his lifelong dedication to music.

© Bayan Northcott, 1998

INTRODUCTION PAR ANTHONY PAYNE

La première fois que j'ai vu les esquisses pour la Troisième Symphonie d'Elgar, c'était à la fin du livre de W. H. Reed intitulé *Elgar as I Knew Him* (Elgar tel que je le connaissais). Une grande partie de ses pages les plus importantes y sont reproduites en facsimilé, et j'étais fasciné immédiatement par la puissance et la vitalité de la musique. Elle jaillissait de la page, et bien que la plupart des esquisses se soient trouvées sur une partition réduite, avec une petite poignée d'indications instrumentales, j'ai tout de suite commencé à entendre les sons de l'orchestre dans ma tête.

Je savais que sur son lit de mort, Elgar avait mis un embargo sur toute tentative d'achever son oeuvre, sur ce qu'il nommait "ses retouches"; mais je ressentais que cela ne pouvait pas m'empêcher de réfléchir à ces esquisses dans l'intimité de ma chambre, et je pris l'habitude de les suivre, aidé par les explications de Reed sur la façon dont il les jouait sur son violon lorsque Elgar l'accompagnait au piano. Pour moi, c'était de la musique qui semblait me montrer Elgar dans un envol d'inspiration, et cela faisait mentir l'opinion reçue selon laquelle il avait perdu toutes ses forces après la mort de sa femme.

L'histoire de la symphonie a été très bien documentée, mais il n'est pas inutile de réitérer les données de base. George Bernard Shaw, un vieil ami d'Elgar, avait souvent harcelé celui-ci pour qu'il produise une troisième symphonie, et il repartit à la charge au début de 1932, en lui suggérant qu'il y avait la possibilité que l'on puisse persuader la BBC de la commander. Elgar mordit presque à l'hameçon cette fois-ci. Il venait d'orchestrer la marche funèbre de Chopin, et lorsqu'un critique lui avait demandé si l'on pouvait orchestrer le reste de la sonate de Chopin pour en faire une symphonie, il avait répondu qu'il allait bientôt en faire une lui-même.

L'histoire prit de plus grandes proportions: les journaux s'en emparèrent, Shaw fit des cajoleries à la BBC, et Elgar affirma même avoir "écrit" la symphonie lorsqu'on le questionna au Festival des Trois Chorales de cette année-là. Les compositeurs peuvent impliquer des choses très différentes, lorsqu'ils affirment avoir "écrit" quelque chose, mais on peut présumer qu'une grande partie de la symphonie était déjà claire dans sa tête. Il ne lui manquait plus qu'un peu de temps pour mettre tout cela sur papier. En décembre, la BBC finit par annoncer officiellement qu'elle avait commissionné la symphonie, et on peut affirmer qu'Elgar accorda un grand sérieux à son oeuvre à partir de ce moment-là.

Au cours de ce qui allait être la dernière année de sa vie, il mit une partie de l'oeuvre sur papier. Parfois, c'était une section assez développée, et d'autres fois tout juste une progression d'accords, et Reed nous raconte ces sessions intenses qu'ils passèrent tous deux sur la musique. Elgar tapait sur le piano à tour de bras, et exhortait Reed à se donner à fond sur son violon. Le compositeur avait une façon de travailler assez extraordinaire, sautant d'un mouvement à l'autre, au gré de ses envies. C'était comme s'il formait les différentes pièces d'un puzzle, avant de les assembler. Les idées lui arrivaient parfois en dehors du contexte d'un tempo, et l'une, par exemple, qui était clairement intitulée scherzo, finit par se retrouver dans le mouvement lent. De la même façon, on remit en service certains thèmes datant des années précédentes en service - les idées pour *Le dernier jugement*, par exemple, un oratorio qui ne vit jamais le jour, et certains épisodes de sa musique secondaire pour le drame historique de Laurence Binyon, *Arthur*, qu'il avait composé une dizaine d'années plus tôt. Les critiques en ont profité pour critiquer sa symphonie, mais on ne voit pas pourquoi on ne pourrait pas réattribuer certaines idées de cette façon, surtout si elles étaient aussi impressionnantes qu'elles le sont ici: cette pratique remonte à Bach et même au-delà. Les thèmes empruntés d'Elgar devinrent une partie de sa vision globale, fusionnés par l'intensité de sa pensée créatrice.

Tragiquement, ces travaux n'allaient néanmoins pas porter fruit. En octobre 1933, après une opération exploratrice, on lui diagnostiqua un cancer, et il se mit à se détériorer rapidement. Il arrêta de composer, et il mourut en février 1934, laissant derrière lui plus de 130 pages d'esquisses pour la symphonie inachevée. Je suis convaincu que ces pages contiennent les vestiges d'une oeuvre inspirée, elles semblent pourtant n'avoir éveillé que très peu d'intérêt jusqu'à relativement récemment. La réputation d'Elgar plongea très bas juste après sa mort qui en serait la raison partielle; mais même lorsqu'on explora ses esquisses, il y eut peu de perspectives imaginatives.

Mon implication personnelle dans cette oeuvre, remontant à la fin de 1972, n'a pas immédiatement conduit à un travail sérieux. La contemplation des esquisses n'était qu'un passe-temps intermittent, et il y eut des années pendant lesquelles je n'y prêtais aucune attention. Mais tout cela changea en 1993. Paul Hindmarsh de BBC Manchester m'appela pour me demander si cela m'intéresserait de donner une certaine forme à ces esquisses pour en faire une interprétation en atelier. J'ai sauté sur l'idée: cela allait me forcer à rassembler mes idées et à écrire systématiquement les nombreux liens de connexion entre les esquisses et leurs extensions que j'avais envisagées au cours des années. Je ne fis guère attention à la mise en garde de Paul, me prévenant que les personnes détenant les droits d'auteurs de ce projet devaient d'abord donner la permission à la BBC: sous l'impulsion de ce moment exaltant, j'ai achevé le scherzo pour lequel les esquisses procuraient tout le matériel, et j'ai ensuite réussi à écrire une exposition complète pour l'adagio en travaillant les esquisses comme les pièces d'un puzzle. Si le livre de Reed m'avait énormément aidé à me souvenir de la séquence des événements dans le scherzo, ce ne fut pas le cas pour l'adagio. Reed ne semblait pas savoir comment s'ouvrait le mouvement, bien que cela soit clair d'après les esquisses, et il n'était pas non plus conscient de l'ordre dans lequel les sujets principaux devaient apparaître. Il fallait décider de tout ceci grâce à des hypothèses.

La BBC m'avait alors envoyé des photocopies des esquisses complètes qui se trouvaient à la British Library, et j'ai découvert que Reed avait négligé un grand nombre de pages d'un intérêt considérable. Armé du morceau, et encouragé par un petit bout de musique du développement que j'avais découvert dans les esquisses complètes, je commençai à avoir une meilleure idée sur la façon de finir l'adagio. Je fonçai en avant et écrivis la dernière mesure le 23 février 1994, ne me rendant compte que plus tard, avec un grand frisson, que ce jour marquait le soixantième anniversaire de la mort du compositeur. A ce stade, je pensais avoir fait tout ce qu'il était possible, car Elgar n'avait écrit que l'exposition et la récapitulation du premier mouvement, alors que la matériau du final ne permettait d'assembler que l'exposition.

Tout ceci allait bientôt devenir un intérêt académique, néanmoins, parce que la famille Elgar, qui contrôlait les droits d'auteurs des esquisses, en vint à décider après maintes délibérations qu'ils ne pouvaient pas permettre de laisser continuer ce projet. Très honnêtement, ils pensaient que l'on ne pouvait pas changer le désir exprimé par leur grand-oncle sur son lit de mort. Je compatissais avec leur point de vue, mais il est évident que j'étais extrêmement déçu. J'avais commencé à m'impliquer dans la symphonie autant que si elle avait été l'une de mes oeuvres.

A ce stade, je remis tout dans le tiroir du bas, considérant avec découragement que je n'allais probablement jamais revenir à la symphonie. Mais la saga eut une suite. La famille n'avait aucune objection à l'idée d'une émission de radio ayant ces esquisses pour sujet, tant qu'il n'y aurait aucune allusion à mon 'retouches'. Je me lançai donc et fis l'enregistrement d'une discussion pour la BBC en mars 1995. Cela causa quelque remous, et convainquit un grand nombre de personnes qui avaient auparavant sous-estimé les esquisses du fait que la symphonie aurait été de la plus grande qualité. Après l'enregistrement, je suis rentré chez moi en pensant que c'était vraiment la fin de l'histoire, mais le destin me réservait d'autres surprises. Le jour suivant, après avoir jeté un dernier coup d'oeil sur les esquisses, et avant de les ranger pour de bon, j'ai découvert très soudainement la clé permettant d'achever le premier mouvement — celle-là même que j'avais reconnue impossible dans ma récente discussion radiophonique. L'idée me frappa avec la force d'un coup de foudre: je me rendis compte qu'il y avait quatre pages de fragments légèrement soulignés que j'avais d'abord rejetés et qui étaient en fait réservés à la section du développement. Prenant le taureau par les cornes, j'ai terminé le développement et son coda associé en une quinzaine de jours. En dépit de l'embargo de la famille, je ressentais que je devais à Elgar de finir tout ce que je pouvais pendant que c'était encore dans mon esprit. La postérité allait peut-être trouver de la place pour ma réalisation, même si les circonstances étaient alors contre ce projet.

C'était maintenant l'été 1995, et j'ai dû mettre la symphonie de côté pour le moment pendant que je finissais l'une de mes propres commissions. Mais après la grisante expérience d'avoir fini le premier mouvement, j'ai ressenti pour la première fois qu'il m'était peut-être possible de finir toute la symphonie. C'était comme si j'étais poussé par des forces extérieures, et le destin reprit le dessus une fois de plus: la famille Elgar commença à changer d'avis. Se rendant compte que les esquisses du livre de Reed allaient de toute façon en 2005 ne plus être protégées par les droits d'auteur, permettant alors à n'importe qui 'd'y faire des retouches', ils se décidèrent à prendre le contrôle de la situation. Il leur fallut quelques mois pour atteindre un consensus, mais ils finirent par arriver à une décision unanime finit par être atteinte, consistant à me commissionner une version complète de la symphonie, et j'ai commencé en août à écrire en partition orchestrale intégrale tout ce que j'avais fait jusque là. C'est-à-dire les trois premiers mouvements et le début du final. C'est en faisant cela que je devins de plus en plus conscient de l'ampleur globale de la symphonie. La pure étendue de ses émotions la rendait différente de toutes ses autres oeuvres symphoniques. Il y avait la vigueur crue et le lyrisme magique du mouvement d'ouverture, l'utilisation d'une certaine légèreté dans le deuxième qui allait bien au-delà de sa pratique établie symphonique, et l'intensité virulente de l'adagio, tragique dans son importation, alors que le final révélait un monde d'action chevaleresque et théâtral.

J'avais tout ceci dans un recoin de ma tête lorsque je dus faire face au dernier et plus grand obstacle: nulle part Elgar n'avait-il laissé un quelconque indice sur la façon dont sa symphonie allait s'achever. J'ai dû composer la totalité de la section du développement et le coda, bien comme dans le premier mouvement, mais sans indications utiles, et j'ai dû envisagé le but ultime de l'oeuvre — mission la plus difficile de toutes — impliquant des concepts visionnaires pour rester fidèle à la bravoure créatrice d'Elgar. Je n'étais même pas sûr de la structure de base qu'Elgar avait en tête pour son final, bien que je ressentais que l'étendue du matériau d'exposition des esquisses pointait vers une forme de sonate. J'ai enrichi cela en incorporant dans le développement un ravissant interlude en sol mineur dont la place dans le mouvement n'est pas indiquée avec précision dans les esquisses. A présent, le passage semble s'être égaré depuis un substratum de rondo et produit une ambivalence structurelle que j'espère digne de la pensée symphonique d'Elgar.

Quant aux pages de fermeture de la symphonie, j'ai décidé de tout oser en l'honneur de l'imprévisibilité d'Elgar. Et s'il avait pensé mettre les répétitions obsédantes de *The Wagon Passes* (La caravane passe) de sa *Nursery Suite* récemment achevée dans un contexte symphonique plus large? Le sujet principal du final suggère en fait cette sorte de traitement, et il allait éloigner la musique vers un monde visionnaire et nouveau, s'étendant sur les années situées entre la mort du compositeur et mon essai de réalisation de ses esquisses. Je fis confiance à mon sens de l'intuition, et je me mis à écrire.

© Anthony Payne, 1998

EDWARD ELGAR

Edward Elgar est né en 1857 à Broadheath, dans le Worcestershire, et il a vécu une grande partie de sa vie à la campagne qu'il adorait; il est mort chez lui à Worcester en 1934. Bien que sa familie ait été musicale, Elgar fut un compositeur entièrement autodidacte, et il commença d'abord à s'établir comme professeur de musique et violoniste professionnel. Les compositions qu'il publia au cours des années 1890 étaient dans la lignée de la tradition de l'oratorio anglais, mais il obtint une renommée internationale avec son *Enigma Variations* pour orchestre en 1899. Il allait revenir à l'oratorio à plusieurs reprises, plus notamment avec *The Dream of Gerontius* (1900), mais il n'acheva jamais la troisième partie d'une trilogie ultérieure sur les Apôtres. Il se tourna plutôt vers les oeuvres symphoniques — les deux symphonies de 1908 et 1911, le Concerto pour Violon (1910), l'étude symphonique *Falstaff* (1913) et en 1919 le Concerto pour Violoncelle. Il était un compositeur très talentueux de musiques plus légères, dont les cinq marches *Pomp and Circumstance*. Après la mort de sa femme en 1920, il n'écrivit guère, bien que les dernières années de sa vie démontrent une tentative de retour à la composition sur grande échelle, dont un opéra. Elgar fut l'un des premiers grands compositeurs à enregistrer sa propre musique, et il dirigea un grand nombre d'enregistrements entre 1914 et 1933, supervisant au téléphone l'enregistrement final d'une session depuis son lit, un mois avant sa mort.

© Colin Matthews, 1998

ANTHONY PAYNE

Compositeur, écrivain et animateur, Anthony Payne est l'un des musiciens britanniques les plus respectés de sa génération. Né à Londres en 1936, il commença à composer alors qu'il n'était encore qu'un jeune garçon — mais après avoir étudié la musique à Durham University, il passa par une phase d'incertitude créatrice, le faisant se débattre pour intégrer les innovations de l'avant-garde venant du Continent avec le romantisme de compositeurs britanniques de début du vingtième siècle tels Elgar, Delius et Vaughan Williams pour lesquels ils ressentaient des affinités. Ce n'est qu'après avoir fini *Phoenix Mass* alors qu'il n'avait qu'une trentaine d'années (1965–72) qu'il finit par ressentir "l'émergence naturelle d'une manière nouvelle, longtemps recherchée mais qui n'avait été envisagée dans le passé que partiellement".

Depuis, pourtant, il a accumulé un catalogue imposant composé d'une cinquantaine d'oeuvres de genres les plus variés, à la seule exception de l'opéra. En plus de ses deux commissions principales pour la série des concerts de la BBC — *The Spring's Harvest* (1985) et *Time's Arrow* (1990) sa contribution orchestrale inclut la paraphrase de Delius, *Spring's Shining Wake* (1981) et les *Orchestral Variations* — *The Seeds Long Hidden* (1994) autobiographiques, alors que ses musiques vocales et de chambre vont du Quatuor à Cordes constructiviste (1978) au sextuor que l'on joue souvent, *A Day in the Life of a Mayfly* (1981).

Pendant ce temps, Payne continue à promouvoir la comprehension de la musique par l'intermédiaire d'un grand nombre d'activités: il est auteur de livres sur Schoenberg et sur Frank Bridge; critique musicale pour le *Daily Telegraph*, *The Independent*, et *Country Life*; il contribue à tout un éventail de publications allant de *Tempo* au *New Grove Dictionary*, il enseigne dans les universités aussi éloignées que l'Australie et les Etats-Unis; et, pour garder le meilleur pour la fin, il anime fréquemment des émissions de radio. En plus de ses longues années de service pour la Société pour la Promotion de la Musique Nouvelle, il continue à diriger le jeune ensemble d'aventuriers, Jane's Minstrels, qu'il co-fonda en 1988 avec sa femme, la soprano Jane Manning, comme une expression pratique de son dévouement de toujours à la musique.

© Bayan Northcott, 1998

EINLEITUNG VON ANTHONY PAYNE

Ich begegnete den Skizzen zu Elgars dritter Symphonie erstmals am Ende von W. H. Reeds Buch *Elgar as I Knew Him* (Elgar, wie ich ihn kannte). Die wichtigsten Passagen werden dort als Faksimile wiedergegeben, und ich war sofort gefangen von der Kraft und Vitalität der Musik. Sie sprang buchstäblich aus der Seite, und obwohl die meisten Skizzen in Particell standen mit nur wenigen instrumentalen Angaben, hörte ich sofort schon in meinem Kopf Orchesterklänge.

Ich wußte, daß Elgar auf seinem Sterbebett ein Embargo über Versuche zur Fertigstellung des Werks verhängt hatte, über das, was er 'Pfuscherei' nannte; ich meinte jedoch, daß mich dies nicht vom Grübeln über die Skizzen in meinen vier Wänden abhalten konnte und ging sie mit Hilfe von Reeds Schilderung durch, wie er sie auf seiner Violine spielte, während Elgar am Klavier saß. Die Musik zeigte mir Elgar scheinbar in inspiriertem Höhenflug und strafte die Meinung Lügen, daß er nach dem Tod seiner Frau zu nichts mehr in der Lage gewesen sei.

Die Geschichte der Symphonie ist gut dokumentiert, es lohnt sich jedoch, die grundlegenden Ereignisse noch einmal zu wiederholen. Elgars guter Freund George Bernard Shaw hatte den Komponisten oft aufgefordert, eine dritte Symphonie zu schreiben. Anfang 1932 wiederholte er sein Anliegen und meinte, daß sich die BBC vielleicht überreden ließe, sie in Auftrag zu geben. Dieses Mal biß Elgar fast an. Er hatte kurz vorher Chopins Trauermarsch orchestriert, und als ihn ein Kritiker fragte, ob der Rest von Chopins Sonate sich zu einer Symphonie orchestrieren ließe, erwiderte er, daß er lieber eine eigene schreiben würde.

Die Angelegenheit wuchs lawinenartig an: Zeitungen griffen die Geschichte auf, Shaw überredete die BBC, und Elgar erwähnte, daß er die Symphonie "geschrieben" habe, nachdem er diesbezüglich beim damaligen Three Choirs Festival ausgefragt worden war. Komponisten können verschiedenes meinen, wenn sie behaupten, etwas "geschrieben" zu haben, wir können jedoch vermutlich davon ausgehen, daß ein Großteil der Symphonie bereits in seinem Gedächtnis verankert war. Was ihm nun fehlte, war die Zeit, sie niederzuschreiben. Im Dezember verkündete die BBC dann offiziell, daß sie die Symphonie in Auftrag gegeben habe, und von da an können wir davon ausgehen, daß Elgar das Werk ernst nahm.

Während seines letzten Lebensjahres schrieb er Teile des Werks nieder. Manchmal war es ein erweiterter Teil, manchmal nur eine Akkordfortschreitung, und Reed erzählt uns von intensiven Sitzungen, die sie gemeinsam über der Symphonie verbrachten. Elgar habe auf dem Klavier gehämmert und Reed angehalten, auf der Geige alles zu geben. Der Komponist hatte eine außergewöhnliche Arbeitsweise, er sprang von Satz zu Satz, wie es ihm gerade gefiel. Es war, als forme er die Teile eines Puzzles, ehe er sie zusammenfügte. Er hatte zum Beispiel manchmal Ideen außerhalb des Kontexts eines Tempos, und eine, klar mit Scherzo überschrieben, fand sich schließlich im langsamen Satz wieder. Zur gleichen Zeit wurden auch Themen aus früheren Jahren verwendet — zum Beispiel Ideen für *The Last Judgement*, ein Oratorium, das nie das Licht der Welt erblickte, und Episoden aus seiner Zwischenspielmusik für Laurence Binyons historisches Drama *Arthur*, das er ein Jahrzehnt zuvor komponiert hatte. Kritiker hielten dies der Symphonie entgegen, es gibt jedoch keine überzeugenden Gründe, warum Ideen nicht auf diese Weise neu zugeteilt werden können, besonders wenn sie so beeindruckend wie hier sind: diese Praxis findet sich schon bei Bach und noch früher. Elgars geliehene Themen wurden Teil einer übergreifenden Vision, zusammengeschmolzen durch die Intensität seiner kreativen Gedanken.

Leider war seine Mühe jedoch umsonst. Im Oktober 1933, nach einer Operation, wurde Krebs festgestellt, und es ging schnell bergab. Er komponierte nicht mehr und starb im Februar 1934. Elgar hinterließ mehr als 130 Seiten von Skizzen für die unvollendete Symphonie. Ich bin der Auffassung, daß diese Seiten die Vestiges eines inspirierten Werks enthalten, dennoch fanden sie bis vor kurzem wenig Interesse. Elgars Beliebtheit nahm nach seinem Tod ab, was zum Teil dafür verantwortlich ist. Aber selbst als die Skizzen untersucht wurden, gab es wenige Einsichten.

Meine eigene Beschäftigung mit ihnen Ende 1972 führte nicht sofort zu ernsthafter Arbeit. Die Betrachtung der Skizzen war bloß ein Hobby und Jahre solten vergehen, in denen ich ihnen keine Beachtung schenkte. 1993 änderte sich dies jedoch. Paul Hindmarsh von BBC Manchester rief an und fragte, ob ich daran interessiert wäre, die Skizzen für eine Workshopaufführung zu ordnen. Ich war von der Idee begeistert: jetzt würde ich gezwungen werden, meine Ideen zu ordnen und systematisch die vielen Verbindungsglieder zwischen Skizzen und Erweiterungen von ihnen niederzuschreiben, die mir im Laufe der Jahre eingefallen waren. Ich schenkte Pauls Einspruch wenig Beachtung, daß die BBC zunächst die Erlaubnis für das Projekt von den Besitzern des Copyright einholen müßte: in diesem erhebenden Augenblick vollendete ich spontan das Scherzo, für welches die Skizzen das gesamte Material enthielten, und es gelang mir dann, für das Adagio eine vollständige Exposition mittels eines Puzzlespiels mit den Skizzen zu schreiben. Reeds Buch, das mir bei der Festlegung der Reihenfolge der Ereignisse im Scherzo äußerst hilfreich gewesen war, nutzte mir nichts für das Adagio. Er wußte scheinbar nicht, wie der Satz anfing, obwohl die Skizzen es deutlich machen. Auch wußte er nicht, in welcher Reihenfolge die Hauptthemen auftreten sollten. All dies mußte mittels Sachkenntnisse und Intuition ausgearbeitet werden.

Die BBC hatte mir mittlerweile Photokopien der vollständigen Skizzen geschickt, die in der British Library lagern, und ich stellte fest, daß Reed viele interessante Seiten übersehen hatte. Mit dem Teil in meinen Händen und ermutigt durch ein Stück der Durchführung, das ich in den vollständigen Skizzen gefunden hatte, sah ich allmählich, wie ich das Adagio vollenden konnte. Ich kämpfte mich voran und beendete den letzten Takt am 23. Februar 1994, mußte später jedoch mit Schaudern feststellen, daß dieser Tag der 60. Todestag des Komponisten war. Ich dachte damals, daß ich alles erreicht hatte, was sich erreichen ließ, denn Elgar hatte nur die Exposition und Rekapitulation des ersten Satzes niedergeschrieben, während es das Material des Finales ermöglichte, die Exposition und nichts weiter zusammenzufügen.

All dies sollte bald jedoch nur von akademischem Interesse sein, denn die Familie Elgars, die das Copyright an den Skizzen hatte, kam nach langem Überlegen zu dem Schluß, daß sie die Arbeit an dem Projekt nicht länger dulden konnte. Sie war der Meinung, daß der letzte Wille ihres Großonkels nicht mißachtet werden dürfte. Ich hatte Verständnis für diese Entscheidung, war jedoch verständlicherweise zutiefst enttäuscht. Ich hatte mich in die Symphonie vertieft, als wäre sie meine eigene.

Zu diesem Zeitpunkt steckte ich wieder alles in die unterste Schublade und dachte ziemlich niedergeschlagen, daß ich wohl nie mehr zu der Symphonie zurückkehren würde. Die Saga ging jedoch weiter. Die Familie sagte, sie hätte nichts gegen eine Radiosendung über die Skizzen, solange nichts von meiner 'Pfuscherei' erwähnt würde. Ich nahm also im März 1995 ein Gespräch für die BBC auf. Es erregte viel Aufmerksamkeit und überzeugte viele, die die Skizzen zunächst unterschätzt hatten, davon, daß die Symphonie von höchster Qualität geworden wäre. Ich fuhr nach der Aufnahme nach Hause und dachte, daß dies wirklich das Ende der Geschichte wäre, das Schicksal wollte es jedoch anders. Am nächsten Tag, als ich einen letzten Blick auf die Skizzen warf, ehe ich sie für immer wegpacken wollte, entdeckte ich auf einmal den Schlüssel zur Vollendung des ersten Satzes - was, wie ich gerade in meinem Gespräch gesagt hatte, ich für unmöglich gehalten hatte. Die Idee traf mich wie ein Blitz. Ich stellte fest, daß vier Seiten von schwach umrissenen Bruchstücken, die ich zuvor nicht beachtet hatte, tatsächlich für die Durchführung bestimmt waren. Ich stürzte mich gleich in die Arbeit und vollendete die Durchführung und die verwandte Coda in wenigen Wochen. Trotz des Vetos der Familie, meinte ich, es Elgar schuldig zu sein, soviel wie möglich fertigzustellen, solange ich den Sinn dafür hatte. Vielleicht hätte die Nachwelt einen Platz für meine Realisierung, obwohl die Umstände zur Zeit dagegen waren.

Wir schrieben jetzt Sommer 1995, und ich mußte die Symphonie beiseite legen, während ich eine eigene Auftragsarbeit beendete. Nach der belebenden Erfahrung der Fertigstellung des ersten Satzes, fühlte ich mich vielleicht erstmals in der Lage, die ganze Symphonie zu vollenden. Es schien, als wären äußere Kräfte am Werk, und wieder spielte das Schicksal mit. Die Familie Elgars begann, ihre Meinung zu ändern. Es wurde ihr bewußt, daß die Skizzen bei Reed im Jahr 2005 sowieso nicht mehr urheberrechtlich geschützt waren und es dann jedem möglich wäre, damit zu 'pfuschen', und so entschloß sie sich, die Sache in die Hand zu nehmen. Es dauerte einige Monate, eh die Familienmitglieder sich einigen konnten, schließlich trafen sie jedoch die einmütige Entscheidung, bei mir eine vollständige Fassung der Symphonie in Auftrag zu geben. Im August fing ich dann an, all jenes in Partitur zu schreiben, was ich bis dahin geschaffen hatte. Das heißt, die ersten drei Sätze und den Anfang des Finales. Während dieser Arbeit wurde ich mir der Bewegung der Symphonie weiter bewußt. Sie unterschied sich wegen ihrer emotionalen Breite von Elgars anderen symphonischen Werken. Es gab die rohe Kraft und magische Lyrik des Anfangssatzes, den Gebrauch einer leichteren Art im zweiten, der weit über Elgars etablierte symphonische Praxis hinausging und die brennende Intensität des Adagio von tragischer Bedeutung, während das Finale eine Welt ritterlicher Handlung und Dramas enthüllte.

All dies ging mir durch den Kopf, als ich mich dem letzten und größten Hindernis gegenübersah; Elgar hatte nirgendwo einen Hinweis hinterlassen, wie seine Symphonie enden sollte. Ich mußte die gesamte Durchführung und die Koda komponieren, wie im ersten Satz, jedoch ohne hilfreiche Tips, und mußte mir das endgültige Ziel des Werks vorstellen — die schwierigste Aufgabe überhaupt, die visionärer Vorstellungen bedurfte, wenn ich Elgars kreativer Kühnheit gerecht werden wollte. Es stand noch nicht einmal fest, welche grundlegende Struktur Elgar für das Finale vorschwebte, obwohl ich meinte, daß die Breite des erklärenden Materials in den Skizzen auf eine Sonatenform hindeutete. Ich bereicherte die Skizzen, indem ich in die Durchführung ein hinreißendes g-moll-Zwischenspiel einfügte, dessen Platz im Satz den Skizzen nicht eindeutig zu entnehmen ist. In ihrer jetzigen Form scheint die Passage von einer Rondo-Grundlage abgekommen zu sein, und bietet eine strukturelle Ambivalenz, die hoffentlich Elgars symphonischem Denken würdig ist.

Was die abschließenden Seiten der Symphonie angeht, entschloß ich mich, alles zu Ehren von Elgars Launenhaftigkeit zu wagen. Was, wenn er geplant hätte, die unvergeßlichen Wiederholungen von *The Wagon Passes* (Der Wagen zieht vorbei) aus seiner kurz zuvor erst vollendeten *Nursery Suite* (Kinder-Suite) in einen größeren symphonischen Kontext zu stellen? Das Hauptthema des Finales legt eine solche Behandlung nahe und würde die Musik in eine neue visionäre Welt führen, die die Jahre zwischen dem Tod des Komponisten und meiner versuchten Rekonstruktion seiner Skizzen umspannen würde. Ich verließ mich auf meine Intuition und schrieb einfach drauf los.

EDWARD ELGAR

Edward Elgar wurde 1857 in Broadheath in Worcestershire geboren und verbrachte den größten Teil seines Lebens auf dem Land, das er liebte; er starb 1934 in seinem Heim in Worcester. Obwohl seine Familie musikalisch war, war Elgar Autodidakt, was die Komposition betraf, und er machte sich zunächst einen Namen als Musiklehrer und professioneller Violinist. Seine veröffentlichten Kompositionen während der 1890er Jahre standen in der englischen Oratorientradition; es waren jedoch die *Enigma Variations* für Orchester von 1899, die ihm internationale Anerkennung verschafften. Er kehrte mehrmals zum Oratorium zurück, — am bemerkenswertesten mit *The Dream of Gerontius* (1900), er vervollständigte jedoch nie den dritten Teil der folgenden Trilogie über die Apostel. Stattdessen wandte er sich symphonischen Werken zu — den beiden Symphonien von 1908 und 1911, dem Violinkonzert (1910), der symphonische Studie *Falstaff* (1913) und 1919 dem Cellokonzert. Elgar war ein äußerst geschickter Komponist leichterer Musik, einschließlich der fünf *Pomp and Circumstance* Märsche. Ab 1920, nach dem Tod seiner Frau, schrieb er sehr wenig, obwohl er in seinen letzten Jahren den Versuch unternahm, zu großangelegten Kompositionen, einschließlich einer Oper, zurückzukehren. Elgar war einer der ersten großen Komponisten, die ihre eigene Musik aufnahmen, und zwischen 1914 und 1933 leitete er viele Aufnahmen. Einen Monat vor seinem Tod kontrollierte er zum letzten Mal per Telefon eine Aufnahme von seinem Bett aus.

ANTHONY PAYNE

Der Komponist, Schriftsteller, Rundfunksprecher und Animateur Anthony Payne ist einer der geschätzten Britischen Musiker seiner Generation. Er wurde 1936 in London geboren und fing als Schüler mit Komponieren an. Nach seinem Musikstudium an der Durham University machte er jedoch eine Periode künstlerischer Ungewißheit durch, als er sich bemühte, die Innovationen der kontinentalen Avantgarde mit der Romantik Britischer Komponisten des frühen 20. Jahrhunderts wie Elgar, Delius und Vaughan Williams zu verbinden, zu denen er sich hingezogen fühlte. Erst mit der Fertigstellung der *Phoenix Mass* (1965–72) mit Anfang Dreißig fühlte er endlich "das natürliche Auftauchen einer neuen Art, seit langem begehrt, zuvor jedoch nur teilweise begriffen".

Seit jener Zeit entstand jedoch ein beachtlicher Katalog von mehr als 50 Werken in allen Genres außer Oper. Neben seinen beiden großen Aufträgen für die BBC Promenadenkonzerte — *The Spirit's Harvest* (1985) und *Time's Arrow* (1990) — umfaßt sein Orchesterwerk die Delius-Paraphrase *Spring's Shining Wake* (1981) und die autobiographischen *Orchestral Variations — The Seeds Long Hidden* (1994). Seine Vokal- und Kammermusik reicht von dem konstruktivistischen Streichquartett (1978) zu dem vielgespielten Sextetts *A Day in the Life of a Mayfly* (1981).

Payne warb weiterhin für Musikverständnis mit einer Vielzahl von Aktivitäten: als Autor von Büchern über Schönberg und Frank Bridge, als Musikkritiker für *The Daily Telegraph*, *The Independent* und *Country Life*, er gab zahlreiche Veröffentlichungen heraus, von *Tempo* bis zum *New Grove Dictionary*, als Dozent an Universitäten in Australien und den Vereinigten Staaten, und nicht zuletzt immer wieder als Rundfunksprecher. Neben jahrelanger Tätigkeit für die Society for the Promotion of New Music berät er weiterhin das junge Ensemble Jane's Minstrels, das er 1988 zusammen mit seiner Frau, der Sopranistin Jane Manning, als praktischen Ausdruck seiner lebenslangen Hingabe an die Musik mitbegründe

CONTENTS

The first public performance of this work was given on 15 February 1998 at the Royal Festival Hall, London, by the BBC Symphony Orchestra, conducted by Andrew Davis.

First recording: NMC D053, by the above performers.

Recording of Elgar's sketches, with narration by Anthony Payne: NMC D052M, by Robert Gibbs (violin) and David Owen Norris (piano); also featuring the BBC Symphony Orchestra, conducted by Andrew Davis.

INSTRUMENTATION

3 Flutes (3rd doubling Piccolo)
2 Oboes
Cor Anglais
2 Clarinets in B♭ and A
Bass Clarinet
2 Bassoons
Double Bassoon
4 Horns in F
3 Trumpets in C
3 Trombones
Tuba
Timpani
*Percussion (3 players)
2 Harps
Strings

*triangle, tambourine, side drum,
bass drum, cymbals, tam-tam

Duration: 58 minutes

Performance materials are available on hire

Music origination by Jack Thompson.

Cover photograph: Sir Edward Elgar, Bt, by Herbert Lambert.
By courtesy of the National Portrait Gallery, London.

Facsimiles of Elgar's manuscript and sketches reproduced
by permission of the Sir Edward Elgar Will Trust.

SYMPHONY No. 3

The sketches of EDWARD ELGAR
elaborated by ANTHONY PAYNE

I

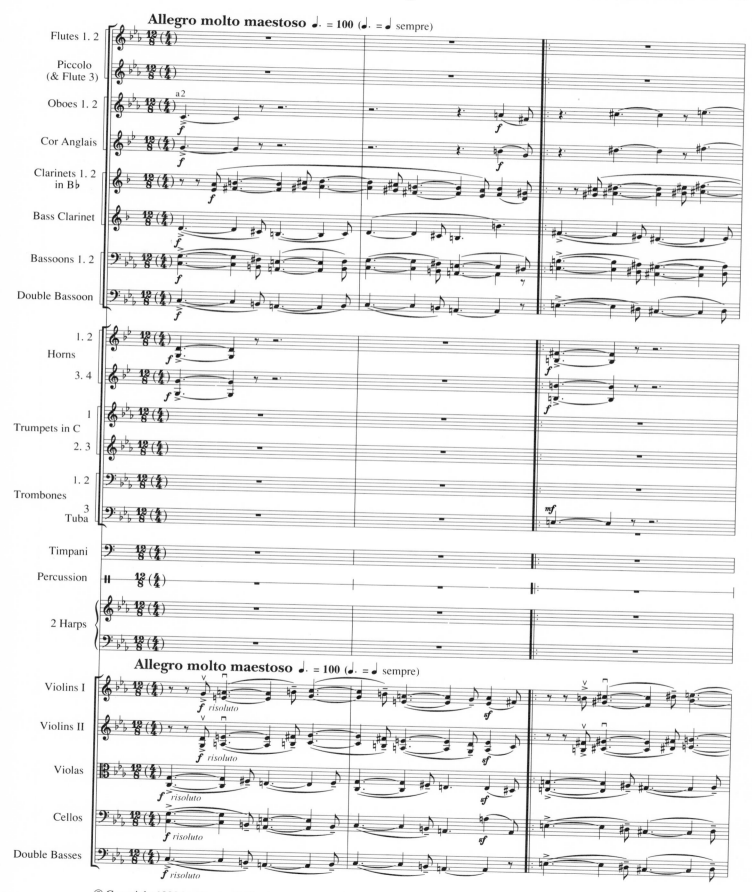

4

10

*) N.B.: Harp 1 plays *both* staves an octave higher.

*) N.B.: Harp 1 plays *both* staves an octave higher.

II
Scherzo

III

*) Senza sord, desk by desk

114

IV

126

304